YOU AND YOUR PASTOR

WHAT YOU CAN EXPECT

MARVIN T. JUDY

ABINGDON PRESS
Nashville

To our grandchildren:
John, Allison, Joseph, Daniel

YOU AND YOUR PASTOR

This book is printed on recycled, acid-free paper.

Library of Congress Cataloging-in-Publication Data

Judy, Marvin T.
Pocket guide to you and your pastor / Marvin T. Judy/

ISBN 0-687-46773-X (alk. paper)

1. Clergy—Office. I. Title. II. Series.
BV660.2.J83 1992
253—dc20 91-42512
CIP

Unless otherwise noted, Scripture quotations are from the King James Version of the Bible.

MANUFACTURED IN THE UNITED STATES OF AMERICA

PREFACE

The pastoral ministry is one of the skilled professions. Denominations are requiring increasingly longer and more intensive training of pastors. Most major denominations now expect a candidate for the ministry to have completed four years of college with a sufficient academic level to do a minimum of three years of graduate study in an accredited seminary. One or two years of in-service training are also usually required as an internship or "trial."

How laypersons should look upon their pastor and how they can best use his or her services is a question laypersons often ask. I spent seventeen years in the active pastorate in both rural and urban churches. Many times I was embarrassed to discover there had been a serious need in the personal life or home of a member of the congregation, and I had not been a good minister simply because I was not aware of the need. During my twenty-eight years teaching in a theological seminary, I was with hundreds of ministers of different denominations, many of whom were serving pastorates, and in this capacity I heard the problems ministers face in their pastoral work. One of the most repeated problems was the difficulty that results when laypersons misunderstand the proper ethics in regard to the use of the pastor's time, and the calling of ministers other than the pastor for special services such as weddings, baptisms, and funerals. Several books have been written on ministerial ethics, but little has been written on "lay ethics" in regard to the proper use of the pastor.

This small work has been prepared to assist laypersons to use the time and services of the pastor wisely. All ministers desire to be of the utmost help to the members of their congregation. It is hoped that a number of the questions laypersons ask will be answered in this writing, and a more efficient use of the services of the pastor can be made by the laity as some of the guides suggested are put into practice.

Marvin T. Judy
Professor of Sociology of Religion Emeritus
Perkins School of Theology
Southern Methodist University

CONTENTS

CONTENTS

The Pastor in Your Illness

Christians have traditionally had a benevolent concern for fellow Christians in times of illness. One of the earliest acts recorded regarding the first-century church was the ministration of the church to widows, the poor, and the "shut-ins." One of the responsibilities of the deacon, a lay office, was to take the Holy Communion to persons who could not attend the worship of the congregation. The entire congregation should continue to have a sense of responsibility for the members of the church, and not leave all responsibility to the pastor. The pastor does, however, have a dedicated role to fill in the time of illness. He or she desires to be of assistance to persons who are ill, and members of the congregation should feel free to call upon the pastor in illness, feeling no encroachment upon their time. Visiting and ministering to the sick are a part of the pastor's duty.

As there are many types of illness, there are varied degrees of pastoral needs in illness. There is the person with an illness of short duration; the illness which requires hospitalization; serious illness which requires weeks or months of convalescing; the illness from which the patient will never recover, but must be bedfast for months or even years; and terminal illness, with the inevitable death which must be faced by patient, family, and friends. It is impossible in this writing to cover all types of situations. Therefore, certain general principles concerning the layperson's use of the pastor will be stated, and specific areas of pastoral roles will be discussed categorically.

Some General Suggestions

Call the pastor. This may sound obvious, but it is amazing how many laypersons expect the pastor to learn of their illness through the "grapevine." Many laypersons have been ill for days and wondered why the pastor didn't call. The truth of the situation was that the pastor did not know of the illness. He or she wants to know the nature of your illness, the seriousness and duration, and what your personal needs are. If your illness is a short one, you may feel no need to notify the pastor. On the other hand, if you would like for your pastor, or another minister in your congregation, to visit with you, tell them. They will appreciate your frankness and judgment.

Share any special concerns with your pastor. If you have worries about your illness share these with your pastor. He or she will want to be of the greatest assistance possible. Your pastor is visiting you as a representative of the church, and you should feel free to disclose any spiritual concerns you may have, including problems concerning your family or finances which may have been brought to an acute stage due to illness.

Don't be hesitant in discussing the nature of your illness, the seriousness of it, or the possibility of death. Pastors are schooled in such fields and can help you to meet your needs. I visited with an elderly lady of the congregation over a period of five years. With each visit she would say, "Please tell me how to die. You know, according to my age I don't have long to live." At the age of ninety-four she passed away. It was always a pleasure, however, to discuss death with "Aunt Sally," for she faced it frankly, without fear, with genuine sincerity, and an abundance of Christian hope.

Many types of illness are aggravated by worries, anxieties, fears, or other attitudinal problems. To share such problems with the pastor may assist greatly in a spiritual and physical recovery.

The pastor is a religious counselor. When the pastor calls at the time of your illness (or at any other time), he or she is a representative of the church. You may "pass the time of day" together in a light, friendly conversation, but your pastor wants to be of help to you in ministering to your religious life. Don't hesitate to share any concerns you have. Your pastor will gladly hear your questions and counsel with you on any basic religious concerns you may have. Prayer is also a part of the life of the ministry. Though he or she may hesitate suggesting it, your pastor will always welcome your request for prayer.

Special services. When one has been ill to the extent

of having to miss the routine services of worship, it is appropriate to ask the pastor to conduct a brief service in your home or hospital room. The service may consist of a Scripture reading, a brief meditation, and prayer. The pastor is always ready to take to the ill or shut-in the sacrament of the Lord's Supper. Many pastors will take the sacrament of the Lord's Supper to the aged or to shut-ins routinely, but the person with a shorter illness will usually need to ask for it. Many congregations record the Sunday services, and a tape can be brought to the home, usually by a layperson.

The length of the call. The usual pastoral call on persons who are ill will be three to five minutes. This will vary according to the seriousness of the illness and the needs of the patient. Should the patient have major problems to discuss with the pastor it may take much longer for the call. The pastor is ready and anxious to help, regardless of the length of time it takes. Most pastors are sensitive to the needs of the patient, the strength of the patient, and whether the visit has accomplished its purpose. The patient should never feel he or she is encroaching upon the time of the pastor when there are major problems to discuss. It may take repeated calls to resolve major problems.

Types of Illness and the Pastor's Ministry

The short-term, nonserious illness. The pastor will want to know of illness in the home even though it is of a short duration and of a nonserious nature. The pastor may wish to drop by while doing routine calls near your home. You may desire to have your pastor call, or you may inform him or her of the illness and suggest that a call is not necessary.

The practice of hospitalizing a person for routine physical examination is quite common. Any hospitalization of a member of your family should be reported to the pastor. The pastor will use his or her best judgment in determining if a call should be made.

The call at the time of an operation. The pastor will want to be with you prior to an operation regardless of how serious it may be. In some cases it will be appropriate for your pastor to discuss the nature of your case with your surgeon or attending physician. In rare cases, the pastor may accompany the patient to the operating room, especially if the surgeon feels the pastor's presence will benefit the patient. The pastor's ministry can be most helpful in assisting the patient to obtain confidence in the doctor and a victorious faith.

In the event of a serious operation the pastor may want to be with the family at the beginning or throughout the operation. He or she will want to keep in touch with the family until the crisis is past.

During the convalescent days in the hospital, the pastor will want to call on the patient with some degree of regularity.

The shut-in call. There are several reasons why people become shut-ins. There is the parent who has an invalid child in the home or an aged parent or spouse who is an invalid. There are aged couples or widowed persons. There is the invalid who will probably never be able to be out of the home. Many pastors establish a routine for visiting the shut-ins. It is difficult to visit such persons more than once a month, and often the calls must be farther apart than that. As a general rule the call on a shut-in is longer than the sick call, usually five to fifteen minutes. The call will most often include the reading of Scripture and prayer. In a sense, the call is a service of worship which takes the place of worship the shut-in person cannot attend at the church.

Some congregations record the service on tape, and this service is taken to the home of the shut-in person. In this case the pastor should not be expected to take the service to the home. This should be done by volunteer laypersons who are willing to give several hours per week to visitation. Many pastors set aside a specific time each week for visiting shut-ins. It is wise, however, for the shut-in person not to expect the pastor at a stated time. The pastor's schedule is constantly changing due to emergencies and various types of meetings.

The terminal illness. Death is the inevitable end of life. The terminal illness usually makes heavy emotional demands on both the patient and relatives. If the illness can be discussed freely it is generally easier for all concerned. There are problems associated with death that should be discussed among family and friends. The pastor is the logical person to turn to for counsel, consolation, and guidance. Discuss with him or her the problems concerning death and the problems that will confront the family after death. The visits of the pastor in this case may need to be frequent and of a longer duration than those during the normal illness. Christian persons should find much strength and consolation in their faith as death approaches. (See chapter on death for further details.)

The Pastor as Counselor

In practically all denominations, theological training includes formal courses and usually some clinical training in pastoral care and counseling. Such training consists of basic studies in psychology, psychology of religion, the problems of grief, anxiety, and human emotions. The student is taught how to recognize the symptoms of various psychological traits such as hypomania, schizophrenia, paranoia, inversion, and so forth. He or she is trained to separate serious problems that need treatment by a specialist from those where normal pastoral care can be of help. Training generally includes study on the relationship between the normal personality and a sound Christian theology. This may include the therapeutic effects of prayer and faith in the healing process.

Clinical training consists of working under the close supervision of trained counselors in hospital situations among the mentally and physically ill.

Training in seminary is not designed to make the minister an analyst, a psychiatrist, or even a trained clinical counselor. It is designed to give a pastor a broad knowledge of illness and some of the basic methods of counseling. It assists the pastor in being equipped to be of great service in the ordinary, run-of-the-mill problems he or she will encounter in the parish ministry.

One of the most helpful parts of pastoral training is being equipped to distinguish between serious mental and emotional problems and temporary emotional strain. The good pastor will recognize when a parishioner is too ill for him or her to be of permanent assistance, due to the pastor's limited training. The pastor will be in a position to help the patient and family know when they need to seek psychiatric care, or even institutional care. The layperson should look upon mental and emotional illness as any other illness and feel no chagrin at having to call upon psychiatric care for a loved one. Many psychiatrists recognize the value of a healthy religious faith in assisting a person in treatment. Pastors can often work with the psychiatrist in leading persons into a normal mental attitude.

The Assistant Pastor

There are thousands of churches in the United States that have grown to a size so large that it is impossible for a single pastor to minister to the congregation. Assistant pastors, associate pastors, visitation pastors, and other staff are employed by these congregations. In these cases, much of the visitation to persons who are sick and shut-in is done by an employed minister other than the senior pastor. Sometimes members of the congregation do not accept an assistant pastor as readily as they do the senior pastor and tend to feel neglected if the senior pastor does not call. An assistant is employed by the congregation to be a minister to the congregation. As such, he or she is ready and capable to fulfill the pastoral responsibilities. Having multiple staff in a local church makes it possible for the congregation to be more ably served by ministers and should be readily accepted by the congregation. There are, of course, times when you feel you must have the services of the senior pastor of the church. In such cases, feel free to call, and your pastor will be happy to be of service.

THE PASTOR AT THE TIME OF DEATH IN THE FAMILY

Death in the family, whether sudden or expected, is a shock. One is seldom ready when death comes, forcing many decisions upon the family in a few hours' time. Who should be notified of the death? When will the funeral or memorial service be held? What mortician should be called? What clothes should be provided for the corpse? How expensive a casket can be afforded? Where will the service be held—church or funeral home? Where shall the burial be? These are only a few of the questions crowding into the minds of those charged with the responsibility of planning a funeral.

If death is the result of an accident or sudden sickness, frustration grips the family, and a thousand "Whys?" crowd into their minds. Sometimes one will say, "Oh, if only we had done it differently"—meaning a different travel plan, a postponed trip, seeing the doctor earlier, or choosing a different doctor or hospital.

Frequently, in the midst of such anxieties and frustrations the family fails to call the pastor. It is your pastor's desire to be with you at the time of your family member's death, or as soon after death as possible. Some suggestions follow from years of ministerial experience.

First, Christian people believe death is a part of

life. It is normal to be born, and death is a part of the process of life. One of the major tenets of Christian theology is the belief in immortality. This doctrine was held by the Hebrews before Christ and by Christ himself, and was given meaning through the resurrection so vividly symbolized in our Easter observance. In this faith the Christian should find it possible to discuss the matter of death freely with family, friends, and pastor.

Discuss freely with different members of the family what each should do at the time of death. Such calm deliberations before the hour of crisis will save the family frustration and make for clear thinking. I knew of a widow who said to her children three years before her death, "When I am gone you will find a letter in my purse giving you instructions for my funeral." The time came, and though she had been chronically ill for some time, her death was sudden, a heart attack. The letter was found by a daughter. There were full instructions for funeral arrangements, even to the hymns she desired for the service and the minister to be used. Needless to say, as her four children and their families gathered from distant parts of the nation, there was a deep sense of Christian victory in the midst of grief which inevitably accompanies death.

So make your plans. Discuss openly and freely the various aspects of funeral arrangements, including how much can be afforded for the funeral, what mortician will be called, where the memorial service will be held, what minister will officiate, where the burial or cremation will be, and many other details.

Some suggestions follow to better inform the layperson concerning customary practices and procedures when death occurs in your home.

Call the Pastor If Death Is Near

Doctors will frequently share with the family when there is only a matter of hours before death. Your pastor will want to know and will want to be with you, if at all possible, at the time of the actual passing. It should be noted that sometimes a person will linger near death for hours or even days. Naturally, the pastor has many duties and may not be able to remain with you for a prolonged period. In this event, ask your pastor to leave the phone number where he or she can be contacted on short notice.

Call the Pastor as Soon After Death as Possible

The pastor should be called whether you are with the person at the time of death or when you first hear of the death. Your pastor will want to share your grief and to be of assistance in your needs. There are some beautiful, brief worship services for use immediately after death. Your pastor can read one of these services, read from the Scriptures, and offer prayer. This is not the time to plan for the funeral service. It is, in every sense of the term, pastoral ministering to members of the family and congregation.

Call the Mortician

The mortician will take the body to his or her establishment for burial preparation. If the person dies in a hospital certain legalities and routines must be performed for release of the body. Sometimes people in the immediate grief over the death of a loved one find such legal procedures extremely exasperating and repulsive, and they may rebel, feeling this is bringing the secular into a sacred time. But death is a legality. It must be recorded with the Bureau of Vital Statistics, and you, as a family member, will be called upon to supply legal information.

A word needs to be said about autopsies. The cause of many deaths is uncertain. Medical science is engaged in constant research, the result of which is a continual extending of life expectancy. An autopsy performed after death might be a means of aiding the doctor to discover information that can be used for the preservation of life for others. Our rational mind says, "By all means there should be an autopsy," but at the time of death our minds often become irrational and we refuse permission. Such examinations are done in cooperation with the mortician, and the body is not disfigured. For the sake of the living and medical science, permission needs to be given for an autopsy. Post mortem examinations frequently reveal hidden causes of death, which may bring a sense of consolation to the living upon discovery of a prolonged ailment or disorder that might have resulted in invalidness or loss of mental faculties or one of the senses.

In making plans for the funeral, ask the mortician to consult your pastor as to time. After the mortician sets the hour for the funeral, then notify the pastor. Your pastor will cancel important engagements or even church business trips for the funeral, but often conflict can be avoided if he or she is consulted first. The place and hour of the funeral should be set as soon as possible after the death, facilitating your pastor's getting it into his or her schedule.

The funeral or memorial service should be planned in counsel with your pastor. He or she will want an opportunity to talk with you about the service. This can be done at the funeral home, in your home, or you can meet in the pastor's office, as you desire. On the rare occasion when a personal visit is not possible, plans can be made by telephone.

It is not the purpose of this chapter to debate the many aspects of the Christian funeral. Lively discussions have been carried on by ministers and theologians as to what is the Christian funeral. There is no unanimity among ministers in this regard. Most denominations have official and unofficial orders of worship consisting of prayers, Scripture selections, and appropriate liturgies. All communities have customs that are deeply ingrained and traditional. Probably no religious tradition is more deeply ingrained and devotedly followed than the funeral. This is especially true in town and country churches across America. Customs, however, are more readily broken in urban areas, giving way to new practices. The Christian funeral is a service of Christian people in worship. Worship is the expression of one's faith drawing near to God and permitting him to witness to one's own experience.

The usual Protestant funeral consists of one or more hymns, Scripture or other liturgical material, prayers, and a sermon. The sermon will vary greatly in different denominations and with different ministers. Your minister will want your suggestions and is anxious to comply with your desires. Keep in mind your pastor is trained in the meaning of worship and can plan a service of worship in keeping with your denominational practices and the customs of the community.

Use of a Minister Other Than the Pastor

One of the most common problems of the layperson is that of calling a minister other than the pastor for the funeral. It is natural that ties are made with ministers through special events in the Christian experience, such as baptisms, receptions into the church, weddings, and funerals. These ties emerge during the crisis of death, and the layperson feels, quite naturally, a source of consolation that comes from a former pastor or another minister with whom there is intimate acquaintance.

The layperson must keep in mind the strict ethical disciplines held by ministers. One of these is that a pastor will not go into a parish other than his or her own to perform a religious duty in keeping with the pastoral office without an invitation from the pastor of that parish. In the lives of clergy members, this problem has reached the point that they refuse any invitation to go into another parish for such duties. This causes embarrassment to the pastor invited, the pastor of your church, and you. There are, however, proper procedures to follow and, in most cases, clergy are more than happy to conform to your desires. These procedures are listed:

A. Discuss freely with your pastor your desire to have The Reverend __________ assist in the service. Your pastor will not feel he or she is being bypassed, but will be glad to comply with your wishes.

B. Ask your pastor to call the minister and extend the invitation on your behalf. This will take any doubt out of the mind of the invited minister, and he or she will feel free to honor your request if schedule permits.

C. Your pastor is in charge of the service. He or she will expect, and you need to give assurance of this, to conduct the service. The visiting pastor will participate in the service at your pastor's planning.

The usual custom is to have the visiting minister deliver the sermon.

By following the above simple procedures, friction and conflict will be avoided. Laypersons can help in allaying any concerns about a pastor's returning to a former charge.

The Post-Funeral Visit

One of the most awkward times of a funeral, for both the mortician and the pastor, is at the grave when the service has been completed. The mortician would like for the family to leave the grave site so employees can close the grave. Some morticians are masters at putting everyone at ease, but more often there is an uncomfortable few moments for everyone. The customary practice is for the minister to greet the family, then friends and relatives follow with their greetings. In some communities it is the custom for the family to return to the home and receive relatives and friends.

If the minister can work it into the schedule, he or she will want to visit you in your home within a few days after the funeral. At such a time, feel free to discuss the deceased, the funeral, or any question you may have concerning death, immortality, and the Christian view of life. Feel free to ask your pastor to pray with you.

Funeral Fees

There is wide disagreement among clergy concerning a fee for a funeral. Customs differ across the nation. There are some areas of the nation where the matter of a fee for a funeral is unheard of, while other areas make it a common practice.

From the point of view of the pastor, a fee is never charged for a funeral. Some denominations, such as The United Methodist Church, have stated in their rules for pastors that a fee shall not be charged. Therefore, if the pastor is given a "fee," it is purely a gift, not payment for services rendered. Laypersons should keep this in mind and never feel obligated to pay for a funeral service. Many pastors have a rather severe self-imposed discipline and refuse any gift, while others will accept it. Attitudes in regard to a fee are dependent on the custom of the community and the policy of the denomination.

If the pastor incurs expenses, such as travel outside the parish to accompany the body to a cemetery at some distance, or if called out of his or her own parish to assist in a service involving travel expense, the family should reimburse this expense. Most ministers do not have travel allowances and travel beyond their own parish may result in actual hardship.

THE WEDDING

Since ancient times the uniting of a couple in matrimony has been made holy by the blessing of the church through the authorized clergy. The minister is ready to assist a couple in preparation for marriage and the wedding ceremony.

Pre-Marriage Education

Most pastors are prepared to assist couples in pre-marriage education. This may be done in classes conducted for couples planning marriage or in personal interview sessions. With the failure incidence of marriage as high as it is, clergy feel obligated to assist couples in getting a good start and building a good foundation for a successful marriage. Some marriage counselors estimate that only 10 percent of the married couples in today's society have a relatively complete adjustment, and as many as 40 percent of the couples remain together only because of the inconvenience of divorce, expense, embarrassment, social pressure, or for the expediency of children. Pre-marriage education is designed to assist couples in understanding the fundamental nature of marriage. Your pastor may use any method in which he or she feels at home and competent to discuss marriage with you. The important factor is to *give the pastor an opportunity to share with you in pre-marriage education.* This means the couple should consult with the pastor weeks in advance of the wedding. Scheduled interviews will be conducted and suggestions will be made by the pastor with regard to literature on marriage and specific problems you may be facing in your adjustments, medical doctors and specialists in marriage to consult, and family you may want to see.

If the couple are of different religious backgrounds, the adjustment problems are increased. Protestant-Catholic, Protestant-Jewish, or two different Protestant church backgrounds each offers separate problems. Literature on mixed marriages can be suggested by the pastor. (An excellent discussion may be found in James A. Pike, *If You Marry Outside Your Faith* [New York: Harper and Bros., 1962].) Your pastor will want to help you work toward a mutual agreement, settling on a church that will be a compromise but not a complete surrender of either party. This may take weeks or months of reading and training, but the results in marital adjustment are well worth the time.

Wedding Protocol

Wedding ceremonies have two basic purposes: (1) to fulfill a legal act in the sight of the law of two persons who have agreed to live together as husband and wife; and (2) to fulfill the religious act of two persons who have declared together under God that they are now to live as husband and wife, and who are asking the blessing of the church upon their union.

The first of these is accomplished by complying with the laws of the state (and sometimes the county) in which the parties reside. State laws vary, and the burden for knowledge of the law rests upon the parties involved in the marriage. Most states have a waiting period between the time of application for a marriage license and the issuing of the license. Some states require some type of physical examination and blood test. After the license is issued, the groom will need to give the license to the minister performing the ceremony. The minister will fill in the license and mail it to the proper county official for recording. The official will mail the proper document to the couple after recording.

The second basic purpose of a wedding, to fulfill the religious act, will vary widely with different denominations. However, most denominations hold marriage as a sacred religious service to be performed by a duly authorized minister of the denomination. The service may vary in length from a few minutes to more than an hour. It must be kept in mind that a wedding is a divine service of worship, and as such, the officiating minister is responsible for fulfilling the expectations of office representing his or her denomination.

Specific rituals for the wedding ceremony have

been authorized by the denomination. The rituals are in keeping with the denomination's historical and theological tradition. Most ministers will be happy to make minor additions to the wedding ceremony at the request of the couple, provided such changes are in keeping with the meaning and intent of the service. The officiating minister should always have the right to reject suggestions made by the couple. This is a responsibility of his or her office.

Under normal circumstances, the wedding should be held in the church, conducted by the pastor or an associate pastor of the local congregation. So-called wedding chapels or popular chapels for weddings tend to place an emphasis upon the wedding which does not have a religious significance. For couples who have a church home (membership in a local church) that is the normal place for the wedding.

In some cases, couples may wish to invite a minister who is not the pastor to assist with the wedding. This is common, since there are certain sentimental associations with a friend, relative, or former pastor of the couple. It may be that a couple cannot be married in their local church, and must be married in another church in another town or city. In any event, it must always be kept in mind that the pastor of a local congregation is the pastor in charge. All arrangements for the wedding should be made through him or her. Any visiting minister will participate in the ceremony at the direction of the pastor.

When asking a visiting minister to assist in a

wedding, proper protocol is to ask the local pastor to invite the visiting minister to assist. This procedure avoids any awkwardness or embarrassment on the part of either the visiting minister or pastor. For the couple to go directly to a minister other than the pastor of the church in which the wedding is to be conducted is poor ethics, and most ministers will feel a keen sense of bewilderment in answering the request. Much embarrassment can be avoided if the simple steps suggested here will be followed.

The Wedding Rehearsal

For a formal or semi-formal wedding a rehearsal is necessary. Your pastor will want to arrange a rehearsal time with you that is convenient for all parties involved. It must be kept in mind that the pastor is the officiating minister, and regardless of how much knowledge of weddings the couple or members of the wedding party may have, the pastor is responsible for conducting the service in the best manner in the traditions of the denomination.

Sometimes a professional wedding director may be employed. Such a person can be of value in planning the wardrobe of the bride and attendants, arranging for the reception, and other details. A professional wedding director is not responsible for the wedding ceremony. This is the responsibility of the pastor. The pastor may want to invite the professional to assist with the wedding procession, directing persons in the proper order down the aisle and before the altar of the church. In some very large churches it is necessary to have a member of the church staff other than the pastor conduct the rehearsal. In this case, the person designated by the pastor is acting for him or her, and the same basic principles of protocol prevail. The pastor will be present for the wedding ceremony, and in most cases, will be responsible for pre-marriage education.

The Wedding Ceremony

The wedding ceremony is a service of worship. As such, every phase of the ceremony should be in keeping with the central purpose of worship. This means the music should be carefully selected from the traditional hymnody of the denomination. There has developed over the past century a repertoire of wedding music which has come from Hollywood musicals. They are sentimental, and in most cases, beautiful love songs, but they are not hymns for services of worship. Your pastor will be happy to assist the couple in selecting fitting music for the service. Larger churches will have a person on the staff in the field of music who will be of help.

Many churches have adopted certain rules and directions for weddings. Such rules and directions give guidance for the use of the church building, use of the organ and organist, what music should be used (and in some cases what music is forbidden), protocol for the wedding party, use of the fellowship hall for the reception, and other directions. The couple should be willing to follow such directives.

The taking of pictures during a wedding should be avoided. Should pictures be desired in the church before the chancel, the wedding party can return to the sanctuary for such pictures after the ceremony. It is very disruptive to the spirit of worship for an amateur or professional photographer to be taking pictures during the ceremony. It must be repeated for emphasis: *the wedding is a service of divine worship.* As such, the pastor is in charge and should have complete freedom to direct the service to make it as meaningful and worshipful as possible.

The Wedding Reception

A wedding reception is for the purpose of giving friends and relatives of the bride and groom the opportunity to greet the couple, congratulate them, and to meet other persons in the wedding party, including the parents and grandparents of the couple. The custom is common to have the reception in the fellowship hall of the church in which the wedding has taken place. Most churches, large or small, rural or urban, now have such a place for a reception. This carries out the basic idea of the wedding being a service of worship and a time of the blessing of the church on the marriage.

Wedding Expenses

It is not necessary for a church wedding to be expensive. A couple and their families should stay within their income. To place emphasis on dress, elaborate floral pieces, and an elaborate reception is to miss the intent of a wedding. It is not a time for the display of wealth, but a solemn occasion of uniting two persons in wedlock with the blessing of the church. There is no need for a family to feel social pressure in regard to doing a wedding like some other family in the church or community. Each family should feel completely free to plan the wedding "trimmings" in accord with their income.

The matter of a fee for the minister is highly disputed among clergy and varies greatly with community customs. A basic principle prevails—namely, the minister is a representative of the church. As such, he or she is supported by the congregation to perform services of the church. Officiating at a wedding is a part of a pastor's responsibilities, and most clergy do not charge for this service. If the minister is given a fee, it should be purely voluntary on the part of the groom, and should be considered a gift, as one may give a gift to members of the wedding party. Inquiry by the couple about community customs, and with the pastor, will clear the matter. Should a pastor be asked to make a more-than-normal trip involving travel, housing, and meals, the pastor should be reimbursed for such expenses.

Post-Marriage Counseling

Very few marriages are without problems. Such problems usually emerge shortly after the honeymoon. Couples are prone to live with problems, and in many cases, separation and divorce occur when difficulties arise. Your pastor wants to be of assistance in helping a couple find mutual adjustments. The couple should feel free to call upon him or her for counsel. Contemporary seminary training includes courses in pastoral care and counseling. Many unhappy marriages could be improved if couples would call upon their pastor, unburden themselves in confidence, and work out their problems through his or her counsel.

Special Problems

Personal Guilt

Guilt arises when one has overtly violated an understood moral standard. Regardless of the intensity or extent of such a violation, or regardless of how others look upon the violation, the individual will have a sense of guilt. Guilt can cause anxiety, defensiveness, loss of memory, instability, and other abnormal reactions. The church stands as the redemptive agent in society. The pastor is the representative of the church and is ready to counsel with persons at any time there is a need.

One should not hesitate to call the pastor when a personal problem arises. He or she will call in your home or at the church office. Many times an open and frank discussion of the problem of guilt can bring to the individual a sense of repentance, faith, and renewal of life. By virtue of the office, the pastor is pledged to maintain confidence and will not divulge to others the problem you share.

In some Protestant churches there is an established procedure for periodic confessions. This is generally done through a period of self-examination, followed by a visit to the church and an interview with the pastor. The person usually receives the

Sacrament of the Lord's Supper following the interview and confession as a symbol of faith and renewal. For many years, the Roman Catholic Church has made periodic confessions available for the parishioner. Through such practices the layperson may find a release from guilt, though, of course, such a practice must not become "routine" to the point of losing its meaning.

In the past quarter century too little emphasis has been placed upon personal spiritual enrichment through prayer, confession, dedication, and service. Much grief and anxiety could be avoided if persons would practice personal dedication and renewal at home, in corporate worship, and in counseling with the pastor.

Personal Problems

The pastor stands ready to listen to your discussion of personal problems and to be of assistance where possible. Frequently, the problem can be readily solved by sharing a problem with an understanding religious counselor. If an immediate solution is not forthcoming, there is value in knowing someone else is aware of the problem, sharing in the attempt to discover the solution, and covenanting in prayer for strength and guidance. Problems may be of personal nature: irritability, despair, the irritation of certain relatives or friends, finances, uncertainty of the future, a major decision, a personal habit that needs to be broken, or many other areas of vital concern. The problem may be one of marriage, relations with one or more members of the family, or a major conflict between husband and wife. The popularity of certain syndicated "heart throb" daily newspaper columns is an indication of the multiplicity of human conflicts in contemporary culture.

The writer could relate many incidents in his ministry where persons under stress either went to him for sharing the problems or he found in his calling that the parishioner was ready to reveal his or her problem. Success in such situations varies according to the size and nature of the problem, and in degree of involvement of the persons concerned. To say the least, the pastor is anxious to be of service in any problem situation.

The Child in Trouble

Parents are often shocked by the conduct of their children when some mores of the home, church, or community have been broken. Infractions may be anything from a minor disregard for parental authority to a major break with civil law. Regardless of the extent and intensity of the infraction, parents usually feel quite helpless in facing the problem.

The pastor is ready to help carry the burden of families in distress. He or she will want to know of the problem and will do everything possible to be of assistance.

It goes without saying that little can be done with a rebellious child until he or she is willing to enter into a counseling situation. The best cure for such problems is preventive measures, such as the maintenance of a healthy relationship with the church and ministry by the entire family. When confidence in the church and ministry has been broken by parents through their own indifferent attitude, it is difficult to restore such confidence in the children.

Parents can suggest to the child in trouble that he or she make an appointment with the pastor. The child should not be forced to see the pastor, but should make the appointment of his or her own free will, or with total consent for the parent to make the appointment. The pastor will do all he or she can to assist young persons. Resistance on the part of the youth may be encountered, but the pastor may reach the youth successfully.

One of the major problems of contemporary society is the young person who has entered into sexual relations prior to marriage, resulting in pregnancy. The shock of such an experience to young people and their parents often results in catastrophe for one or more of the parties. Shame, grief, frustration, and thwarted dreams are suddenly thrust upon parents and families involved. Every family feels this sort of thing will not occur, yet statistics show that no culture or economic status of society misses the problem. When a problem of this nature arises, the pastor should be called immediately and the difficulty shared with him or her. You will find a sympathetic listener, and one who will enter into the problem. Your pastor will assist in counseling with the couple and will arrange with the couple and family for a wedding, if this is to be the solution. If marriage is not the answer, the pastor is in a position to introduce the girl to social and church agencies that will assist her until the baby is born. The pastor can also assist in counseling with regard to whether she should keep the child or make it available for adoption, and in helping to orient the girl back into normal life. Young persons need to accept responsibility for sexual relations. The father of an illegitimate child needs to accept responsibility for the child and provide support and help in making decisions regarding the care of the child.

Pastoral Calling

There is probably no phase of the pastoral ministry where there is as widespread disagreement among ministers and laypersons as there is with regard to pastoral calling. Traditionally, the Protestant clergy has accepted as part of their responsibility the "visitation from house to house." With the increasing size of congregations and the increasing demands upon the time of the pastor, pastors are compelled to rethink how they can use their time wisely in regard to calling on the laity. Denominational executives responsible for assisting local church committees in securing a pastor state that one of the basic expectations of such committees is "We want a pastor who will call."

This chapter is designed to clarify various types of pastoral calls to assist the layperson in understanding more fully how the time and services of the pastor may be used wisely to a mutual advantage. There are several different types of pastoral calls. Some of these have been touched upon in previous discussions, but will be mentioned here for clarification.

The Sick Call

Pastors are always available to call in the home or the hospital at the time of illness. The extent of the call and the type of visit must be determined by the nature, duration, and seriousness of the illness. This has been discussed in the first chapter.

The Shut-in Call

Shut-ins are persons who are confined to their home, a rest home, retirement village, or hospital for a sustained period of time. The person may be confined to the care of an invalid child, a family member who is sick, or an aging parent. It may be a person who is comparatively young with an incurable malady, or one who requires a long duration in convalescence. It may be a person in mature years who is crippled, ill, or not sufficiently ambulatory to leave the home.

The pastoral call in shut-in situations will be of such a nature that it offers the ministry to the person confined. It needs to be periodic with a fair degree of regularity. Laypersons should let the pastor know of such needs, and the pastor will work regular calls into his or her schedule. Many large congregations will have a person on the ministerial staff with special assignment in this area of ministry.

The "New Baby" Call

Most pastors will want to call on the couple who have just become parents. The call can be brief, with a moment of devotion led by the pastor seeking God's blessing upon the child and asking for guidance for the parents. If the denomination to which the couple belongs practices infant baptism, the parents should discuss the service with the pastor, planning for a date and clarifying the meaning of the service. Call the pastor when a new baby is born.

The Call at the Time of Death

The role of the pastor at the time of death has been discussed in the second chapter. It suffices here to state that the layperson should always call the pastor when death appears imminent, or has come. The pastor will want to call to assist the family in their immediate needs. Later, he or she will need to be consulted in regard to arrangements for the funeral and will want to call in the home a few days after the funeral.

The Evangelistic Call

The pastor in the contemporary church spends a large part of his or her time calling upon persons who need to make a confession of faith or who need to transfer their church membership. Much of the work in this area of the life of the church can be done by laypersons, but the pastor is responsible for final decisions. New families in the community need to be contacted, persons in families connected with the life of the church who have not yet entered into church membership need to be cultivated for the Christian faith, young people need to be led to a personal commitment to Christ and the church, and persons in the community who have not accepted the Christian faith need to be contacted.

The Church Business Call

Much of the pastor's time is spent in visiting with laypersons in the church to discuss the business affairs of the church. The church school superintendent; chairperson of the official board, the session, or other official bodies; the president of the women's organization; the president of the youth organization; men's groups—all leaders of the church must be contacted periodically by the pastor. Many contacts are made at the church office. Many are made at the place of business or the homes of the parties involved. Laypersons should use the time of the pastor for such business calls wisely.

The "Routine Visit" Call

Probably the most controversial aspect of pastoral ministry comes in the area of routine visitation by the pastor. By routine visitation, we mean the pastor's calling upon members of the congregation with some degree of regularity without any specific purpose in mind. Some laypersons expect such calls; others do not.

In the contemporary church there is usually so much activity available for the layperson and so many contacts the pastor makes with laypeople in business activities of the church that many pastors feel a routine call is not necessary. The larger the congregation, the more difficult it is for the pastor to make routine calls. Two aspects of ministry need to be kept in mind: (1) In any given congregation approximately one-third of the membership at any one time is involved in leadership positions, leaving two-thirds without any type of pastoral attention except in times of crisis; and (2) within the Protestant denominations the vast majority of congregations have fewer than five hundred members, making pastoral contacts on a routine basis feasible. Such calls assist in making the services of the pastor and congregation meaningful to each member of the congregation, and they are usually greatly appreciated. The pastor is ready to be a "good shepherd of the flock."

Your Pastor as Your Spiritual Director

The disciples had observed Jesus in prayer. As Christ came from prayer, one of them said, "Lord, teach us to pray, as John taught his disciples." Jesus' response was "When you pray, say . . . " followed by the Lord's Prayer, now known by millions of persons the world over. He then gave two brief parables illustrating the nature of God and prayer. The first of these was the man who went to his neighbor in the night asking for bread for his children, and he received bread. Jesus then made the profound statement, "So I say to you, ask, and you will receive; seek, and you will find; knock, and the door will be opened to you. For everyone who asks receives, those who seek find, and to those who knock, the door will be opened." The second parable followed: "Would any father among you offer his son a snake when he asks for a fish, or a scorpion when he asks for an egg? If you, bad as you are, know how to give good things to your children, how much more will the heavenly Father give the Holy Spirit to those who ask him!" (Luke 11:1-13 REB).

Growth in spiritual understanding is an essential part of the Christian experience. Personal and individual understanding and use of prayer is at the center of growth in spiritual formation. Since the early centuries of Christianity, the priest has served as a spiritual director. A spiritual director in Christian tradition is one who is schooled in theology and has a personal understanding of prayer. He or she is able to assist the inquiring Christian in the understanding of the relationship of prayer, Christian theology, and the Bible and beliefs, and assimilating these into Christian stewardship of time, talents, and service. This role of the priest and the pastor can be traced throughout the Christian era with specific formation in the fourth and fifth centuries in the Desert Fathers in Egypt, Syria, and Palestine. These were priests who devoted their lives to prayer and the spiritual guidance of believing Christians. These persons, in a sense, were "fathers," who helped individuals shape their inner lives through prayer. Literature reveals the felt necessity for individual Christians to have a spiritual director. This would be a person experienced in prayer who would enter into conversation with the individual. His task would be to call to the attention of the individual temptations and overt sinning, and to direct him or her into confession, repentance, faith, established habits of discipline, and service.

The "spiritual exercises" then came into being, consisting of repeated prayers and disciplined praying. One of the first prayers was "O, God, make speed to save me: O Lord, make haste to help me." The "Jesus Prayer" came into being about the fourth century, with the exhortation to repeat it often: "Lord Jesus Christ, Son of God, have mercy on me, a sinner." It was suggested that this prayer be coupled with frequent observance of the "Sacrament of the Lord's Supper."

One of the most effective forms of spiritual direction was the class meeting of the Methodist movement in Europe and America. Two to twelve persons met as a class under the direction of a class leader. Weekly class meetings consisted of prayer, self-examination, confession, and renewal. The annual "protracted" meeting, or "revival," with ten days to two weeks of services each night, and often services and Bible study in the day, brought persons to confession and new dedication.

All Christians need to be in self-examination and rededication. Growth in the Christian experience comes as new areas of consciousness emerge which need to be brought into the orbit of dedication. Growth requires personal prayer, meditation, contemplation, self-examination, repentance, and acceptance of the new life in Christ. It is the never-ending search for "let this mind be in you, which was also in Christ Jesus" (Phil. 2:5). Your pastor is anxious to assist you in reaching this goal. Routine attendance at Sunday church services is a strong means of assisting in the growth process. Corporate worship is the assembling of persons of like mind under the lordship of Christ. "It is the redeemed and redeeming fellowship in which the Word of God is preached by persons divinely called, and the Sacraments are duly administered according to Christ's own appointment. Under the discipline of the Holy Spirit the Church seeks to provide for the maintenance of worship, the edification of believers, and the redemption of the world" (*The Book of Discipline of The United Methodist Church* [Nashville: The United Methodist Publishing House, 1988], p. 19).

The liturgies of the usual church service are designed to assist the worshiper to enter into the presence of God. This is done through call to worship, singing of hymns, prayers of confession, declaration of one's faith, repeating one of the traditional creeds, the pastoral prayer, anthems, and a call to renewal. The sermon is a means of new learning and growth in knowledge. Many personal problems are spoken to in the sermons. Doors are opened through the sermon for conversations with the pastor.

Church school classes provide a means of learning and growth. Much fellowship and support are offered through persons of like mind and desires. Wholesome recreation is designed around the needs of the class members. Special Bible and theology courses are offered for growth in knowledge. The church and church school make possible the witness to the gospel through mission; evangelism; worship; stewardship of time, talents, and possessions; education; and social action.

Your pastor wants to be of assistance as your "spiritual director." This may not take the form in traditional practice of regular times together for council and guidance, but in his or her own way, there is a presence and help when needed.

In recent years much literature has been published dealing with prayer as a means of personal strength, growth, and inner healing. Ministers are trained in seminary to combine the fields of Christian theology and practice with counseling, psychology, and medicine. These services are available for laypersons. Ministers differ in their abilities as counselors and spiritual directors. Each has his or her self-image in their fields. The layperson needs to work with the pastor as he or she feels at home with professional skills.

Four books are listed below for consideration for further reading.

Maxie Dunnam, *Alive in Christ. The Dynamic Process of Spiritual Formation*. Nashville: Abingdon Press, 1982. Dr. Dunnam is former editor of *The Upper Room* and is at this time a pastor. The book is an interpretation of the doctrine of justification by faith and elements making for spiritual growth.

Dwight H. Judy, *Christian Meditation and Inner Healing*. New York: Crossroad Publishing Company, 1991. Dr. Judy is an ordained minister in The United Methodist Church, and at this time a professor and licensed counselor. The book combines theology and psychology with specific directions for establishing and maintaining the devotional life.

Morton T. Kelsey, *Psychology, Medicine, & Christian Healing*. San Francisco: Harper & Row, 1988. Dr. Kelsey is an Episcopal priest, teacher, and pastor.

Kenneth Leech, *Soul Friend: The Practice of Christian Spirituality*. San Francisco: Harper & Row, 1980. Dr. Leech is an Anglican priest, pastor, and professor.

Three Authorities: Laity, Clergy, Denominational Executives

Within each local congregation are three authentic authorities. The laity is the church and has every right to express its authority in decision making. The pastor or clergy has authority of the ordained ministry and is by office "pastor in charge." Each local congregation is a part of a denominational structure that has executives who have certain responsibilities for the local church, pastor, and fulfillment of denominational expectations. Each of these authorities is described in some detail, and suggestions are made for their most effective use within the local church.

Lay Authority

The major concern of the laity is the development of the individual church member in Christian growth and expression. The current theology of the church may be expressed in the following statements: The purpose of the professional employed staff in a local congregation (pastor, associate, minister of education, music, etc.); organizational structure; buildings and equipment; and the connectional system of the denomination is to assist the laity to be the church in worship, nurture, and at work in the world. This doctrinal statement implies: (1) It is the individual Christian in a congregation who develops into the church. The structure of the congregation within the denomination, provided with ministerial leadership, makes possible meaningful individual corporate worship, nurturing in the Christian faith and pastoral and corporate care, and expressing the faith in work in the world. This involves conduct, discipline, and individual involvement in society. (2) The pastor (and employed staff in a large church) is to be the teacher of the faith, exhorter for a disciplined Christian life, stimulator for action, minister and counselor in crisis experiences, director of worship, and representative of the congregation in community and national affairs. (3) The connectional system represented in the offices of denominational executives, regional and national, is to assist the laity to have ministerial leadership and to find a full expression of faith in world mission. (4) Buildings and physical equipment are, in reality, "tools of the trade" to assist in getting a job done.

Laypersons are anxious for their local church to be a success. Success, as they understand it, may be in depth of genuine Christian growth, expansion, education, evangelism, or social action, or it may be a shallow measurement of just good attendance at services and "all bills paid."

Through the past three decades there has been a rise of lay participation and an increasing amount of lay involvement in the life of the church. This is a healthy situation. In keeping with our basic theological statement above, *the laity is the church.* The authentic church and the authentic layperson are a congregation of individual Christians who sense the responsibility for the church in worship, nurturing, and at work in the world. How does the layperson conceive the task? How can the authority of the Holy Spirit be freed within the layperson? How can one work in Christian commitment within the organized body of the church? How can one work with the pastor? How does the layperson express congregational desires to the pastor? How is the corporate body of the church and the individual layperson assisted by the denomination at large, and the nearest denominational representative, to fulfill the Christian mission?

Some congregations are adapting well to the new discovery of the laity in major leadership. Others are troubled. In some cases the struggle with a conflict of authorities becomes so intense that there is a division within the church and a splinter group forms a new congregation. Laypersons have been known to withdraw from the church or become frustrated in feeling the pastor was too slow, too liberal, or too conservative. At times the denominational policies were likewise out of keeping with individual concepts of what the expression of Christianity ought to be.

The basic question is how can the layperson really be the church with authentic authority in a structure where there are two figures of authority in leadership—namely, the pastor and the denominational executive?

Pastoral Authority

In most services for the ordination to the ministry these words are read, "Take thou authority." This authority is for the administration of the Word, sacraments, and order. This is for preaching, administration of the sacraments and the Lord's Supper, and church administration. The pastor has a sense of calling to the ministry. He or she has devoted many years to preparation, usually four years of liberal arts, and three years in seminary. The pastor is elected or assigned to a congregation, and by authority he or she is "pastor in charge." This deserves further elaboration.

"The secret call," that inner persuasion one feels when God challenges for the ministry, gives to the minister a sense of divine authority. It is an awesome thing to feel the presence of the Holy Spirit in one's life, wooing, persuading, assuring one of the secret call of God for ministry in the church. As I have worked through hundreds of autobiographies of ministerial candidates on "My decision to choose the ministry as a life vocation," I have felt I was on holy ground. God does witness to the inner persuasion for ministry. This may be a gentle, growing conviction, or a radical instantaneous vision. The essence of the secret call, regardless of how it is manifested, is *assurance.* With this assurance comes authority.

A second source of authority is knowledge. The contemporary minister must be a person of knowledge. The minister is the teacher of the Bible, theology, and the relationship of theology to all of life. Such knowledge is derived from formal training in university and seminary and continuing education. The minister must be a person of the Bible, the source of recorded authority. There must be systematic theology that can be translated into lay language and made relevant to all of life. The minister must be versed in church history, which is God's action in time. The skills of the profession must be mastered: administration, preaching, counseling, educational methods.

A third factor is the authority of the church. The sanction of the denomination upon the ministry is generally placed through ordination. Ordination is as old as Hebrew and Christian history and is symbolic of a body of people investing authority in a leader in whom they have confidence that God has endowed with the ability to be a leader in their group. This may be a simple tribal ritual or an elaborate investiture ceremony in a major denomination. In Christian history, the authority is for preaching the Word, administering the sacraments, and for administration (order). Ministers do not take ordination lightly and guard its privileges with stewardship responsibility. Ordination is granted to one with these attributes: (1) A feeling of inner persuasion that God has "called" one to ministry. (2) A recognition by one's peers in a local church that there are talents and abilities which lend themselves to the ministry. In The United Methodist Church this recognition comes in a local church in the Charge Conference's recommending one of its members for "license to preach." (3) Training for professional ministry, consisting, in most Protestant denominations, of a four-year liberal arts degree and three years of professional graduate training. (4) A period of trial in ministry is expected in which the potential minister demonstrates his or her ability to perform responsibly in the office of minister.

The authority of integrity is a fourth factor. The word *integrity* is defined as "uprightness of character, probity, honesty, unimpaired state, soundness, completeness, fidelity, justice, virtue, and worth." These are characteristics that should be reflected in all professed Christians—lay and clergy. There is no double-standard. All are responsible for dependability in character and action. In spite of the above statement, there is a "double grief" when a minister succumbs to temptation, bringing a question upon his or her personal life and ministry. In some aspects the temptations of the ministry are the same as those of Jesus. Jesus' first temptation was how he would use his authority. There is always the temptation to simply be a social activist—turn stones into bread and feed a hungry world. This is a noble goal, and in a world where there is an abundance of poverty, a just distribution of the world's goods is vitally important. This the Christian world must do! But "Man does not live by bread alone." Ministry is for the whole of life, as well as for physical well-being.

The second temptation of Jesus was to use his office for a demonstration of the spectacular. Showmanship does not need to consist of "leaping from the church steeple." It can be accepting the spoils of the office. It may be seeking the higher places in the church for self-aggrandizement rather than for a larger place of service.

The third temptation is to "sell out" to less important factors of ministry. For Jesus it was to become a political ruler. This led Jesus to define his own ministry as servant rather than ruler. "I am among you as one who serves" (Luke 22:27 NRSV). "The servant is not greater than his lord" (John 13:16). "He who would be greatest among you, let him be a servant" (Mark 10:44, paraphrased). In each case, the Greek word for "deacon" is used where we translate "servant." *Deacon* may be literally translated, "waiter of tables." A servant is one who is in the role of "waiting" on others. This is the humiliation of the ministry, but also the salvation of the ministerial office.

The fifth factor is "earned authority." Assigned authority is that authority which comes from a position. A pastor is "pastor in charge" by the authority of the denomination, ordination, and being appointed or elected to the office. This authority lasts, however, only as long as it is demonstrably earned. One earns authority through humility, integrity, hard work, quality preaching, meeting the pastoral needs of persons in the congregation, and the ability to influence, to a certain degree, the life of the community.

Authority of the Denominational Executive

Each major denomination has some system of evaluating the work of the clergy. This may be by hearsay in a congregational type of church government, or a rigid process of data storage and computer analysis to match ministerial type and characteristics with certain congregational needs. In The United Methodist Church this responsibility is placed in the offices of bishop and district superintendent.

Presumably, the denominational representative has firsthand information about the pastor, the potential pastors for a congregation, and the specific needs of the congregation as a change of pastors is considered. The executive is also the liaison between the local church and the church at large. Each congregation needs to bear its share of the benevolent and missional concerns of the denomination. Each congregation needs a conscious awareness of the extended church in mission, evangelism, education, worship, and social action.

The denominational executive is the liaison between a pastor and his or her placement, whether this is an election by a local congregation or an appointment by a bishop. A pastor has the right to discuss pastoral opportunities for a change of pastoral charge. The denominational representative is responsible for hearing the congregation's needs in regard to the type of pastor they would like to have. The human relations factors are highly complicated.

The Agreement of Authorities

In the light of the discussion above, it is necessary that the three major areas of authority—the congregation, the pastor, the denominational executive—overtly devise a means of coming to an agreement. Each of the three has major concerns. These are: (1) The concern of the congregation that the pastor fulfill to the best of his or her ability the congregation's needs and expectations for ministry. (2) The concern of the pastor that his or her concept of the ministry shall have full expression within the congregation. (3) The concern of the denominational executive that the pastor and the congregation be "connectional" in their relationships and fulfill the expectations of the denomination.

It is suggested that planned meetings be held for open discussion. The denominational executive will need a free-flowing discussion with the pastor out of which will come an agreement as to the pastor's expectations for ministry, and the expectations of the church at large. The denominational executive will also need discussion with the proper congregational committee to determine the expectations of the congregation, and likewise, their responsibility within the denomination. The proper committees within the local church will need extensive conversation with the pastor, coming to an agreement as to their pastor's self-image and understanding of his or her ministry, and the expectations of the congregation. A retreat for this purpose would be appropriate. (For United Methodists the committees would be the Pastor-Parish Relations Committee and Administrative Board.)

After conversations with hundreds of ministers, and many laypersons, I have devised a series of areas for suggested discussion. These have been tested in numerous situations in local churches, and with denominational executives. They are purely suggestive, and each person involved will need the freedom for input.

There are six basic principles of leadership underlying this process. (1) The work of the church is for the development of persons: laity, pastors, denominational executives. (2) Persons tend to support ideas they have had the opportunity to help formulate. (3) Persons who are affected by a decision need to have a voice in making that decision. (4) Each individual or group conceives of his, her, their potentials, and should have the opportunity to put them into practice. (5) It is the responsibility of each person or group to create a climate for maximum expression of talents and abilities within the framework of defined goals and objectives. (6) Periodic responsible evaluation of work completed is essential. This is done in the light of understood goals and objectives.

Some Guides for Conversation

I. The image of the minister.

1. How do you conceive of the work of the ministry in the congregation?

2. What are the meaningful goals for the pastoral ministry?

3. What are the meaningful goals that the laity conceive for their pastor?

4. What is the place of the laity in "ministry"?

5. How can we assist each other—pastor and laity—to a maximum release of our talents and concepts of ministry?

II. The place of worship in the church.

1. What are our concepts of worship? What is the place in private life, family life, and the corporate body of Christ in the local congregation?

2. What is the chief function of the pastor in worship?

3. What are our concepts of "innovation" in traditional worship?

4. What do we expect the sermon to do for us in worship? What is the place of the sermon in the concept of the pastor? Of the laypersons?

5. In what ways can the laity assist in helping the pastor to maintain a high level of sermon quality and relevance to the needs of the congregation?

III. The place of pastoral responsibility.

1. How do we look upon the position of the pastor in the visitation program? This can be conceived in the following categories: to the elderly; to the shut-ins; to persons who are sick; to persons in distress; to persons having moral problems; to couples having marital problems; to youth who are getting involved in immoral crises; other.

2. How much responsibility for visitation should be shared by trained groups of laypersons? Which responsibilities are those of the pastor only?

3. What do we expect in pre-marriage education (counseling)? How can the laity prepare the congregation for the pastor's role in pre-marriage education?

4. What additional training does the pastor feel he or she needs for pastoral ministries? How can the laity assist in obtaining such training?

5. What are the roles of the pastor and laity at the time of a death in the congregation? Is there a need to establish procedural principles in this regard?

IV. Evangelism.

1. What are our concepts of evangelism?

2. What will our plan be for training children, youth, and adults for church membership? How much of the responsibility is the pastor's and how much the laity's?

3. What shall our program of evangelism be for the coming year?

V. Administration.

1. What are our concepts of the pastor's place as "pastor in charge" and as an administrator? (List the concepts of the pastor and the laity and attempt to bring them into accord.)

2. What responsibilities that the pastor is carrying in administration need to be carried by the laity?

VI. Community and social action.

1. What do we understand to be the place of the church in involvement in the community? (This conversation could be centered around the pastor's concepts and the laity's concepts for local issues, race relations, war and peace, environmental control, and political issues.)

2. What do we understand to be the place of the pastor in community and social issues?

3. What potential areas of conflict do we see due to personal positions held by the pastor or laity in regard to involvement in social issues?

VII. Personal life of the pastor.

1. What areas of personal development does the pastor wish to stress during the coming year? How can the laity assist in providing a climate for this development?

2. What are the suggestions the pastor has to make in regard to the living conditions provided by the church?

3. How does the pastor feel about his or her salary and other financial remunerations in the light of training, years of service in the ministry, and colleagues in ministry of about equal rank?

4. What can be done by the laity to assist with any financial areas which need attention?

5. Are there any areas concerning the pastor's family which laypersons want to discuss?

VIII. Connectional involvement.

1. How do the pastor and laity look upon the pastor's involvement in the connectional and ecumenical aspects of the church? (Conversation can hinge around the obligations the pastor has for sharing connectional interests on the regional and national level.)

IX. Current year objectives.

Most local congregations need to set some goals and objectives for the current year. This should be done in conjunction with the proper organizational structure of the church (e.g., administrative board or similar body). Some areas for consideration are: evangelism, membership, missions, training in each age level, enrichment of personal life, outreach in the community, building and equipment needs, others.

X. Assistance.

In general, are there any ways the laity can be of assistance and greater service to the pastor and to the congregation in fulfilling their mutual ministries?

A Concluding Thought

When the above process has been followed, all three parties or groups will have a greater depth of understanding. The basis for evaluation will not have been imposed by a church body, committee, or individual, but will have emerged out of mutual concerns of the congregation, the pastor, and the denominational executive. The same format may be used by the denominational executive and the pastor. It may also be used in a large church with the senior minister and various members of the church staff adapting the areas of discussion to the various positions of the staff, such as minister of education, minister of music, minister of evangelism, minister of visitation, church business administrator, and secretaries. When a careful record of the conversations is preserved, it will provide a "sounding board" for evaluation of the progress of the church at the end of the church year.

Ministers are different. They differ in their personalities in their self-image, and their concepts of ministry. They differ in their motivations for choosing the ministry as a life vocation, and that may differ from the concepts for the ministry of persons in the congregation. It behooves all persons involved to be tolerant and accepting of one another.

POSTLUDE

All baptized Christians are in ministry. Professional persons employed by the congregation to be their minister(s), buildings and equipment, organizations, the connectional church, are for the purpose of assisting the laity to be the church. Each layperson is the church in worship, nurture, and at work in the world. Professional ministers are set apart through ordination to lead the congregation in worship, to assist members in continual religious growth, and to assist persons in investing their lives in the outreach of the church to persons and causes in need around the world. The congregation is a caring body of persons who look after the needs of one another in love. The professional ministry shares in this concern and lends professional service to the congregation in all stages of life and death.

The Church's one foundation
Is Jesus Christ her Lord;
She is His new creation
By water and the word:
From heav'n He came and sought her
To be His holy bride;
With His own blood He bought her,
And for her life He died.
(Samuel J. Stone, 1839–1900)